CHARLIE CHAPLIN

CHARLIE CHAPLIN

GENIUS OF THE SILENT SCREEN

Ruth Turk

Lerner Publications Company · Minneapolis

Lerner Publications Company
A Division of Lerner Publishing Group
241 First Avenue North
Minneapolis, MN 55401 U.S.A.

Web site: www.lernerbooks.com

Library of Congress Cataloging-in-Publication Data

Turk, Ruth 1917–
   Charlie Chaplin : Genius of the silent screen / Ruth Turk.
     p. cm.
   Includes bibliographical references and index.
   Summary: Traces the life of the legendary film star, from his impoverished childhood in England through his years of success in motion pictures in the United States to his exile in 1952.
     ISBN 0-8225-4957-3 (alk. paper)
     1. Chaplin, Charlie, 1889–1977—Juvenile literature. 2. Motion picture actors and actresses—United States—Biography—Juvenile literature. 3. Comedians—United States—Biography—Juvenile literature. [1. Chaplin, Charlie, 1889–1977. 2. Comedians. 3. Actors and actresses.] I. Title.
PN2287.C5T77 2000
791.436'028'092
[B]—DC21
                                        96-47589

Manufactured in the United States of America
1 2 3 4 5 6 – JR – 05 04 03 02 01 00

Contents

Charlie was born into a family of performers. His mother's stage name was Lily Harley.

 ONE

A Born Performer

1889–1894

On a damp, chilly London night, five-year-old Charlie Chaplin clasped his mother's hand tightly. He quickly propelled himself along, keeping up with her nervous pace. Charlie knew that Hannah Chaplin did not want to be late for her performance at the music hall. If the show didn't start on time, the crowd would become rude and noisy. Charlie had frequently seen patrons hiss and jeer at entertainers who displeased them. Sometimes, if a few spectators had had too much to drink, they would throw rotten fruit and old shoes onto the stage.

Music halls, also called vaudeville, were a popular form of entertainment for working people in England at the time. Shows consisted of various types of entertainment. In a single night, music hall audiences would be treated to singing, dancing, pantomime, and especially slapstick—a type of comedy featuring horseplay, pranks, and other physical humor, such as pie-throwing.

Charlie Chaplin's mother was a singer. Onstage, she was known as Lily Harley. Audiences loved her dainty appearance and her sweet, delicate voice. This night, however, Hannah's throat felt dry and scratchy. The damp weather had irritated her vocal chords, and she worried that she might sing badly. With both Charlie and his nine-year-old brother, Sydney, to care for, she had better be able to sing—or there would be no supper for any of them.

As soon as they entered the back door of the music hall, Hannah Chaplin dropped her son's hand and hurried to the dressing room to put on her costume. Though the backstage area was cluttered with props and performers moving in every direction, Hannah was not afraid to leave Charlie on his own. Charlie's parents had first brought him to the theater at age three, and he had become accustomed to wandering around backstage. The stagehands and entertainers always smiled at the polite, neatly dressed child. Often they paused in their frantic preparations to greet him with a pat on the head. Sometimes they gave Charlie a cookie or piece of candy to nibble on. Most of the time, Charlie stood quietly in the wings, watching his mother perform.

Charlie spent so much time listening to his mother sing that he had memorized her entire repertoire. He also learned other performers' songs, not just because it seemed to make his time backstage move faster, but also because he enjoyed the words and the music.

Born in London in 1889, Charles Spencer Chaplin felt loved and protected. But on this night in 1894, everything changed. As his mother came onstage in her long ruffled skirt and velvet jacket, the usually noisy audience became still and quiet. Lily Harley started to sing. As she reached for the high notes of a beautiful ballad, her voice suddenly cracked.

A rude customer began to whistle. Lily tried again, only to fail once more. She broke down in tears and looked to the music hall owner for help, but he ignored her and darted backstage. To Lily's surprise, he then dragged out her son, who had been watching unhappily in the wings.

Encouraging Charlie to sing any song he wanted, the desperate man waved Hannah off the stage, where she collapsed in the arms of a sympathetic performer. As the small boy advanced bravely to the center of the stage, the unruly audience stopped booing and stared in astonishment. No one knew what to expect from such a young performer.

Vaudeville shows were often rowdy.

Early vaudeville performers often created characters and played them show after show.

Charlie took advantage of the brief lull and began singing a popular melody called "Jack Jones." The way he moved his shoulders and strutted around like someone much older delighted the crowd. They broke into a roar of appreciation, applauding the bold little performer. Charlie gave them one song after another—songs he had spent many hours listening to from the wings of the theater. The songs told sad as well as funny stories. People in the audience also knew the songs well, and they joined in on the choruses, clapped their hands, and stomped their feet.

Soon Charlie started to dance, imitating the dancers he had seen on the stage. Though he had no musical accompaniment, he lifted his feet and tapped and stomped to his own beat, making up the steps as he went along. Charlie even concluded his performance with an imitation of his mother, letting his voice crack in the middle of a song just as she had. The audience screamed with laughter.

Suddenly Charlie felt something sting his cheek. He was terrified, thinking the customers were throwing things at him. They were. Delighted with the boy's performance, the audience flung coins onstage, requesting more songs. Charlie was glad to comply. He was enjoying himself. He collected all the money, then went on with his act until his mother picked him up and carried him off the stage.

Hannah Chaplin never appeared on stage again. Her music hall career was over, but that night a new performer was born. At age five, Charlie Chaplin had made his debut.

Londoners often had to find whatever odd jobs they could to make enough money to survive. This poor family has resorted to selling goods on the street.

TWO

Tough Times

1894–1898

Now that Hannah Chaplin could no longer work at the music hall, she was forced to support her family some other way. Charlie Chaplin Sr. had left his wife and two children years before, and he rarely sent them any money. Hannah sold her jewelry, but the money did not last long. To save on rent, the Chaplins moved into a tiny one-room apartment. Hannah had made her own costumes for many years. Using her sewing skills, she started making dresses for wealthy women to earn some extra money.

Hannah also sewed clothes for her two growing boys, but since she couldn't afford new material, she fashioned outfits for Charlie and Syd from her old costumes. When Charlie arrived at school wearing red stockings sewn from a pair of Hannah's tights, his classmates teased him horribly. Syd received similar treatment when he wore a winter coat made from a velvet jacket with striped sleeves. His classmates described him as "Joseph and the Coat of Many Colors."

The first five years of Charlie's life had been comfortable and secure. He had never gone hungry until his mother lost her job. Hannah tried her best to prepare proper meals, but often the family had little to eat. Some days all they had to eat was a cup of tea and a few pieces of bread. To comfort himself, Charlie would sometimes play an old violin that an actor had given him backstage at the music hall.

Despite their cramped quarters, Hannah was determined to keep her boys as warm and cheerful as she could. On cold, rainy winter days she would put aside her sewing and entertain her children by singing and dancing. Sometimes all three of them would sit at the apartment's single window and observe the passersby. Hannah and the boys would make up stories about the lives of these strangers, trying to imagine where they had come from and where they were going. Sometimes Hannah even acted out the stories in pantomime, never speaking a single word aloud. With her shining blue eyes and delicate features, Hannah Chaplin was talented at silently expressing thoughts and emotions. Charlie and Syd showered their favorite performer with hugs and kisses as well as hearty applause. For a little while, the shows helped them all ignore their very hard life.

Some days, though, Hannah did not feel like singing or acting. She began to get painful headaches and had to lie down with tea-leaf bandages over her eyes. Charlie tried to take care of her while his brother sold newspapers after school. Though Syd earned little money, he kept the family from complete starvation.

One day while Syd was selling newspapers on a bus, he found a purse lying on a seat on the bus's deserted upper deck. Glancing quickly inside, he saw no name or address, only a lot of loose change. Without counting the money,

Sydney closed the purse and ran all the way home. Hannah was lying ill in bed, but when her son dumped the purse into her lap, she sat up. She emptied out the loose change, then noticed a middle pocket inside the purse. She opened it and found seven glittering gold coins, called sovereigns. The value of an English sovereign was about five dollars, and seven of them amounted to more money than any of the Chaplins had seen at one time.

The boys were filled with joy. Hannah announced that since the purse contained no identification, God must have

When Charlie was a boy, many Londoners lived in crowded tenement buildings.

Southend was a popular resort. On this particular day in the early 1900s, a flotilla of warships was on parade.

sent it to them as "a blessing from Heaven." She decided that the family deserved a trip to the seashore.

Not caring that the money would soon run out, Hannah outfitted her sons with brand-new clothes. Then they went off to Southend-on-Sea, a popular seaside resort outside the city of London. At the beach, they kicked off their shoes and ran splashing into the water. They sat on the sand under a huge umbrella, ate ice cream and pastries, and drank lots of lemonade. At night they feasted on a delicious seafood dinner and watched sailboats ride the waves.

The day was a delightful adventure for Charlie and his brother, but it was over all too soon. The family returned home with just a few shillings, only to learn that Hannah's rented sewing machine was being taken away. She had not kept up her payments. The money she had squandered on their vacation could have been used to pay for the machine. Her only source of income was gone. In poor health and unable to care for her children, Hannah Chaplin moved her family to the Lambeth Workhouse, an institution for the poor and the homeless, better known as the poorhouse.

When Hannah told the boys where they were going, they tried to lift each other's spirits by saying that their new home would be better than living in one stuffy room. They tried to think of the move as an adventure. But as soon as they passed through the workhouse gates, Charlie was shocked to learn that he would be separated from his family. After receiving workhouse clothes, Hannah was sent to the women's ward, Sydney was placed with the older boys, and Charlie went with the younger children.

A few weeks later, Charlie and Sydney were moved again, this time to a school for orphans and needy children at Hanwell, twelve miles outside London. Again the two boys were separated. Only six years old, Charlie didn't understand what was happening. At the Lambeth Workhouse, he had at least known that his mother was nearby. At Hanwell he felt alone and deserted.

While Hanwell was a clean and modern school, the rules were strict. Meals were small, clothes skimpy, and children were punished for the slightest offense. Every Thursday a bugle sounded in the playground. While the boys stood at attention, a teacher used a megaphone to shout the names of those who had to report for punishment. One day Charlie's name was called. He could not imagine what he had done wrong. He was charged with setting a fire in the washroom.

Charlie had been in the washroom while some boys were lighting fires on the floor there. But Charlie had not joined in the activity. When asked if he was guilty, however, Charlie was so nervous that he didn't know what to say. He soon felt three sharp blows of the cane on his rear end. He wanted to cry out, but he managed to control himself. When Sydney learned about his brother's punishment, he cried. Because he was working in the kitchen, Sydney was able to sneak an extra roll and butter to Charlie.

Charlie suffered other humiliations at Hanwell. He developed a case of ringworm (an infectious skin condition) and had to have his head shaved, smeared with iodine, and covered with a large kerchief. Then Charlie was confined to a special ward with other infected children.

Another time, one of Charlie's teachers saw him writing with his left hand. At the time, many people thought left-handedness was an abnormality that needed to be corrected. The teacher immediately rapped Charlie sharply across his knuckles. When he kept using his left hand, the punishment continued until his knuckles became swollen and bruised. So Charlie learned to write with his right hand. For the rest of his life, Charlie could write with either hand, but he never forgot the painful lesson.

At Christmas, Charlie suffered the worst punishment of all. Because he had forgotten to make his bed on Christmas Day, he didn't receive gifts of fruit and candy like the other children. He had never felt so unloved and alone.

After eighteen months in the workhouse, Hannah tried to set up a home again. In January 1898, the two boys went to live with their mother, but they were still desperately poor. Fortunately, Hannah was able to rent another sewing machine and sewed women's blouses. The family lived behind a pickle factory and near a slaughterhouse. The smells were awful, but at least the family was together again.

In school, Charlie found himself far behind his classmates. But he won them over by performing "Miss Priscilla's Cat," a humorous speech that his mother had taught him. Although he was just a young boy, Charlie knew that he wanted to become an entertainer.

As a boy, Charlie was already an engaging entertainer.

THREE

Lucky Breaks
1898–1910

Though Hannah tried hard to keep her family together, her headaches returned and she had to be hospitalized. The child welfare authorities decided that Charlie and Sydney should be sent to live with their father. Charles Chaplin Sr. had once been a successful actor and mime, but a serious drinking problem kept him from performing.

The court ruled that the boys must live with their father, but the arrangement did not work. Charles Sr. lived with a woman named Louise, who liked to drink as much as he did. She treated the boys badly. When their father was sober, Charlie and Sydney enjoyed listening to him talk about his performing days, but this was rare. Most of the time the apartment rang with the terrifying sound of loud shouting and drunken fights.

After a few months, Hannah was able to leave the hospital, and the boys returned to their mother once more. For a while, Charles Sr. sent Hannah money, but this gesture did not last long.

One day in 1898, when Charles Sr. happened to see nine-year-old Charlie on the street, he realized that he had not been a very good father. He tried to think of a way to help his son and decided to talk to his friend William Jackson. Jackson managed a group of young clog dancers. Called the Eight Lancashire Lads, Jackson's troupe was popular in London's music halls. Charlie did not have much experience with clog dancing—a style similar to tap dancing, except that performers wear heavy wooden shoes. But his father recommended him so highly that Jackson hired the boy immediately to fill a vacancy in the troupe.

Charlie was excited about this lucky break, but he was also nervous. Jackson insisted on perfect coordination and timing from his dancers. But after several weeks of intensive training and rehearsal, Charlie could dance as smoothly as the other boys.

For the next two years, Charlie appeared on stage with the Eight Lancashire Lads. Although Jackson occasionally enrolled the young dancers in schools, Charlie's formal education was over. Instead, he learned from watching other performers, noting which moves drew special appreciation from the audience. As pay, Charlie received room and board, plus half a crown (about a dollar) a week—a good sum of money for a young performer new to the business. Charlie sent the money home to Hannah.

In 1900, the Lancashire Lads toured the towns around London, then played the famous London Hippodrome in a Christmas show called *Cinderella*. Charlie played a cat, wearing a bulky mask with moveable eyes. He added a comic touch by approaching a dog's rear end and sniffing—a move that wasn't in the script. When the audience laughed, Charlie turned and winked one of the mask's large eyes. In the wings, the stage manager made frantic gestures for Charlie to stop, but Charlie ignored him. The audience roared with laughter and applause. Charlie was only eleven years old, but he loved being the center of attention.

While Charlie was growing as a comic, his brother Sydney went from job to job. He worked as a messenger for the telegraph office and finally signed up as a bugler on a ship bound for Africa. His job was to blow the bugle three times a day to call the sailors to meals and ship drills.

On May 7, 1901, while Sydney was at sea, Charles Chaplin Sr. died from complications of his alcohol abuse. Charlie never knew his father well, but he still felt the loss. Shortly afterward, his mother's mental and physical health began to deteriorate.

The sight of his usually lively and cheerful mother staring quietly out the window for hours at a time was almost more than Charlie could bear. Their once tidy little apartment grew dusty and neglected, and Hannah's behavior grew strange and unpredictable. Sometimes, when Charlie went out, Hannah wandered around the neighborhood, handing out lumps of coal to children as birthday gifts.

Charlie did his best to care for his sick mother, but it was more than a young boy could manage. His job performing with the Lancashire Lads had ended, so Charlie worked as an errand boy, a doctor's helper, and a glassblower, but he did not keep any of these jobs for long. Finally, he bought flowers at the market and sold small bouquets in taverns. Customers saw his sad dark eyes and the black mourning band he wore on his arm to honor his father. Many people felt sorry for Charlie and bought his flowers.

One afternoon in 1903, Charlie returned home to find Hannah in a worse state than ever before. He knew she could

Charlie chopped wood to support himself. These young men are chopping wood in a workhouse.

no longer be left alone. Charlie took her to the hospital, where a doctor told him that she needed long-term treatment for mental illness. Hannah Chaplin was admitted to the Cane Hill Asylum. Charlie returned to an empty room to wait for Sydney's ship to come home.

Lonely and hungry, Charlie roamed the streets of London. He didn't know when his brother would return or what would happen to his mother. To add to his worries, Charlie had no money to pay the rent. The landlady allowed Charlie to stay without paying but warned him that he would have to move out of his room if someone else wanted it.

One day Charlie met a group of woodchoppers who gave him some work. With the few coins he earned, he bought some bread and cheese and had a meal with the friendly workers. That night, when Charlie returned to his room, the landlady gave him a telegram. It was from Sydney, asking Charlie to meet him at Waterloo Station the next morning.

Sydney was shocked to find Charlie so dirty and hungry. As a bugle blower, Sydney had earned twenty British pounds (about sixty dollars). So he paid his younger brother's rent, bought him new clothes, and fed him a good meal. Afterward, the boys went to the hospital to see their mother. She hadn't improved. Sydney and Charlie realized she could not come home. They were still on their own.

The boys knew that if they were thrifty, they could manage on Sydney's earnings for the next few months. Sydney thought he might like to be a performer, too, so the brothers decided to visit theater agencies together and ask about trying out for shows. One agency contacted Charlie shortly after his visit. The Blackmore Agency was casting for a new play called *Sherlock Holmes,* and there was a part for Charlie in the role of Billy, Holmes's young assistant.

At age fourteen, Charlie was slight, short, and fine-boned. He had curly dark hair, expressive dark eyes, and straight white teeth. On the surface, he appeared reserved and shy.

When Charlie was handed the script, he nearly froze with fear, thinking he was expected to read it right then and there. Charlie could not read very well and was relieved when he was told to study the script at home and report back in a few days. With his brother's help, Charlie learned his lines fast. For three days, Sydney read the script aloud to him for hours at a time. At the end of the third day, Charlie had the script perfectly memorized.

With Charlie in the role of Billy, *Sherlock Holmes* opened at London's Pavilion Theatre on July 27, 1903. The play had a successful run in London and then went on tour to different cities. Charlie persuaded the directors to give Sydney a small part in the show so the brothers could be together. Young Sydney convincingly played the role of a middle-aged aristocrat.

With the beginnings of new careers, the Chaplin boys were more confident. For a little while, Hannah's health seemed to improve. She was delighted with her sons' success and was even able to join them on a few of their tours. The brothers' combined earnings made it possible for them to afford an apartment in a better part of town. After Hannah was allowed to leave the hospital, she tried to maintain a home for her boys when they were not on the road.

Another break came for Charlie and Sydney when they met Fred Karno, a clever entertainer renowned for his work in slapstick comedy. Karno had been the first music hall performer to combine pantomime with music. His company, the

At fourteen years old, Charlie debuted in the play Sherlock Holmes. *His name is circled.*

Fred Karno was one of the most influential men in the music hall business.

Fred Karno Speechless Comedians, was one of the most successful comedy troupes in England.

Karno saw the Chaplin brothers perform one night in *Sherlock Holmes* and was so impressed by Sydney that Karno offered him a job with his troupe. In a few months, Sydney Chaplin was doing so well in the troupe that he decided to approach Karno about a job for his brother.

When Charlie arrived for his interview, Karno thought, "he looked much too shy to do any good in the theater, particularly in the knockabout comedies." Much to Karno's surprise, however, the quiet boy spoke up, informing the director that he was seventeen years old and had lots of experience. Karno responded that Charlie didn't look seventeen. When Charlie shrugged and said defiantly, "That's a question of make-up," Karno reconsidered and gave him a small part in the show.

Charlie went to great lengths to make an impression. Feeling that his small role was not exciting enough, he exaggerated the part, adding tricks and gestures, such as twirling a skinny cane, wearing shoes several sizes too large, spinning his little black hat up in the air, and turning somersaults. Charlie's pranks delighted the spectators. Some of the other actors in the show were upset that the newcomer was getting laughs, but the more applause Charlie received, the more he carried on.

Recognizing Charlie's unique talent for comedy, Karno gave him larger parts in later shows. In 1909 Karno took the entire troupe to Paris. He chose Chaplin to play an important role at the Folies-Bergère, a theater famous for its extravagant musical productions. *Billboard,* a magazine that published theater reviews, called Charlie's performance "perhaps the funniest act ever to hit vaudeville."

When Charlie was nineteen, he fell in love for the first time. Hetty Kelly was a pretty dancer in one of the acts in Karno's show. Hetty was also attracted to Charlie, but she was only fifteen, and her protective parents broke up the relationship as soon as they learned about it. Charlie was crushed. It took him a long time to get over his romantic feelings for Hetty.

Over the next few years, with Karno's encouragement and advice, Charlie began to add little sentimental touches to his performances. In addition to acting silly, he often acted frustrated or sad. Audiences could sympathize with his character, and they cheered for him when the shows had a happy ending. Charlie discovered that when he mixed in a few tears with the laughter, audiences found the combination irresistible. This technique distinguished Charlie from most comedians, who relied strictly on slapstick and jokes.

As Charlie's performances received more acclaim, Karno gave him a substantial raise in salary. In 1910, when Charlie was twenty-one, the director invited him to join the company for a tour of the United States. Charlie soon befriended Stan Laurel, another young comedian in the troupe. Charlie and Stan were thrilled about going to the United States. Neither of them knew what lay ahead in the country across the Atlantic Ocean.

A joking Charlie sets sail for New York on his first tour to the United States.

FOUR

The Little Tramp

1910–1914

Charlie's American tour began in New York City in 1910. At first, life in New York made Charlie homesick for London. As he walked along Broadway at night, however, the bright lights and dazzling billboards gave him a pleasant sense of adventure. The warm breeze of a late summer heat wave felt good against his cheeks.

The Karno company appeared in New York in a show called *The Wow-Wows*. American audiences did not appreciate British humor, however, because Americans liked broader comedy—with more stunts and pratfalls. The show was not a success. Though Charlie received favorable notices for his act, he felt humiliated and dejected like all the other performers.

Trying to forget this disheartening situation, Charlie went browsing in secondhand bookstores. He thought he might try a course of self-improvement and invested in a few grammar textbooks. But he only opened them a couple of times before putting them at the bottom of his trunk. Instead, he discovered novels by noted American writers such as Mark Twain, Edgar Allan Poe, Nathaniel Hawthorne, and Washington Irving. Rather than socializing with other performers, he often read in his dressing room between shows. Though he had been a poor reader as a boy, Charlie began to enjoy reading and learning about the United States from American authors.

One evening, while playing to a mostly English audience in a theater on Fifth Avenue, *The Wow-Wows* cast received a standing ovation. The performers were thrilled—especially when an agent attending the show booked the company for a twenty-week tour through Canada, the Midwest, and California.

Fred Karno changed the title of the show, as well as some of the material—to make it more appealing to American audiences. With its fresh approach, *A Night in an English Music Hall* was a success. Once again, Charlie received excellent reviews for his part in the show. He performed a pantomime, playing a polite drunk who tries to preserve his

While in New York, Charlie played a drunk called The Inebriate in A Night in an English Music Hall.

dignity while falling in and out of the cardboard boxes that he's trying to pack. The act required the skill of an acrobat, and Charlie's agile movements and ridiculous expressions induced gales of laughter.

When the tour was over, the company sailed for London. Charlie did not know when he would return to the United States, but he hoped it would be soon. He liked the fast pace of American life, and he felt encouraged by the way American audiences had responded to him.

Back in London, Charlie found that his brother had married and that his mother's condition had grown much worse. The brothers could afford to move Hannah to a private hospital, where she would receive the treatment she needed.

Married life kept Sydney busy, so Charlie did not see his brother often. Alone and sad, Charlie longed to return to the United States. For a while, he found work in several London music halls, but he felt restless and unhappy. A few months later, when Fred Karno announced another American tour, Charlie eagerly signed up.

Charlie was thrilled to find himself back in the United States. As the Karno Company traveled across the country by train, stopping to perform in small towns and big cities, Charlie and the others got to meet many different kinds of Americans. Farmers, ranchers, executives, and schoolteachers all came out to watch the comedians perform in local theaters.

The long train rides between towns gave Charlie hours to practice playing his violin. He also read a lot of books. But his solitary behavior made some of the other actors think that Charlie was a snob. In reality, he was just very shy and didn't make friends easily.

When the tour reached Philadelphia, Charlie received a telegram from New York. He was puzzled to see that the telegram came from a movie agent representing Mack Sennett, director of the famous Keystone Comedies. Charlie had never met Mack Sennett, but Sennett had remembered seeing the English comic perform in New York in 1911. He had been impressed with Charlie's unique act. Now, two years later, there was an opening in the Keystone Film Company. The director wanted to offer Charlie a contract.

The Keystone studio produced short, silent movies that relied on slapstick, car chases, and clownish makeup to get laughs. These early films didn't have recorded music, songs, or spoken words, because sound recording had not yet been perfected. Instead, when the films played in movie theaters, a piano player or organist was paid to sit up front and play music to accompany the on-screen actors. Words of written dialogue, called titles, were also flashed on the screen to help audiences follow the story.

Charlie had seen a few Keystone Comedies, but he didn't know if his personal brand of comedy belonged with the pie-throwing and slapstick for which Keystone was famous. He also didn't know if he should give up a fairly successful career for something unknown. But movies were brand new. Charlie decided that the opportunity to make more money in a new and exciting field was too tempting to resist.

The Keystone Company turned out movies quickly—at the rate of one per week. Like other studio bosses of the silent film era, Mack Sennett had complete control over the scripts, actors, and studio staff. As a contract actor for Keystone, Charlie would be required to play any role in any film he was assigned. He could not choose his own parts or take a job with another studio.

In May 1913, Charlie arrived in Hollywood, California— center of the film industry. His first sight of the Mack

Keystone's actors rarely rehearsed or followed a script.

Sennett studio shocked him. The dilapidated old buildings that had once been part of a farm didn't look like any movie studio Charlie had ever imagined. Outside in a large field, several large movie sets stood side by side. Four or five films were being produced—all at the same time! A row of movie cameras cranked away while directors shouted commands, actors threw pies, dogs barked, and flashlamp powder and cigarette smoke choked the air.

The more Charlie watched, the more confused he became. He couldn't imagine performing on one of those noisy sets. Charlie's style of acting depended on careful planning and rehearsal. Any noise or movement around him would be disturbing. From what he saw on the huge outdoor lot, nothing at all appeared planned or rehearsed.

For two days, Charlie went to the Mack Sennett studios but couldn't work up the courage to enter. On the third day, Sennett phoned, wanting to know where Charlie was. Mumbling an excuse, Charlie nervously returned to the studio. The director told him that the day's filming was ready to begin, but when Charlie asked for a script, he was told that there wasn't one. Sennett would be making up the story as he went along. All this was new to Charlie. He listened to the orders shouted at him, but trying to follow them was another matter. Without realizing it, Charlie kept moving out of camera range and wrecking the entire scene.

Sennett wondered if he had made a mistake in hiring Charlie. He told Charlie to take a few days off to study Keystone's moviemaking methods. Charlie knew Sennett was disappointed in him. He made up his mind to show his new boss he could do the job he'd been hired for. Watching and listening closely, he moved from set to set, trying to master the strange new system, which seemed to consist of nothing but frantic car chases, tossed pies, and manic tumbling thrown together in one scene after the next.

One afternoon as Charlie stood in the background watching Sennett direct a film, the director saw him and beckoned. To Charlie's surprise, Sennett told him to put on some makeup and get into the scene. When Charlie asked what costume he should wear, the director told him to put his own costume together.

Charlie had only a few minutes to get ready. The wardrobe room overflowed with a crazy assortment of hats, shoes, jackets, and wigs of every size, shape, and color. Charlie knew he was expected to look funny, but he didn't want to look like everyone else.

When Charlie walked out of the wardrobe room onto the set, everyone turned to look at him. From his tiny bowler hat to his enormous shoes (worn on the wrong feet), Charlie's ensemble was hilarious. He wore baggy old pants and an ill-fitting jacket, accompanied by a toothbrush mustache and a skinny cane. As Charlie walked, he turned his feet outward, shuffling along while twirling the cane.

Sennett was impressed. Never before had he seen a comedian invent a character right before his eyes. Charlie had created a marvelous portrait of a hobo, down on his luck but still struggling to be a gentleman. Sennett knew it would not be easy to fit Charlie's style of comedy into Keystone's, but he went ahead, hoping to turn Charlie into a star.

In February of 1914, Charlie's first film, *Making a Living,* premiered. The film was only fifteen minutes long, but the public was delighted with the comedian's antics. This movie was followed a few months later by *Kid Auto Races at Venice.* To

This costume turned Charlie into one of cinema's best-loved characters.

make the film, Sennett had sent Charlie to Venice, California, site of a children's auto race. Charlie was told to wear his hobo costume and make a nuisance of himself at the track while the camera operator filmed the event. This movie lasted only five minutes, but once again audiences loved it.

In his third film, *Mabel's Strange Predicament*, Charlie was paired with Mabel Normand, a popular comic actor. She was the first performer to throw a pie in the movies. Charlie and Mabel made a great comedy team. They successfully combined on-screen romance with slapstick routines. Charlie wore his hobo outfit in all three of his first pictures, but movie-goers did not seem to tire of it.

But Henry Lehrman, a director who worked for Sennett, didn't think the English comic really fit into the fast-paced Keystone Comedies. He told Sennett that Chaplin was too slow and that he belonged on the stage instead of in the movies. By this time, however, Charlie was fast becoming a favorite with the public.

Silent films did not give credit to the actors on the screen. Most studios feared that once an actor became a star, he or she might demand too much money. But the more movie audiences saw of Charlie, the more they clamored to know the identity of "the Little Tramp." With his ludicrous suit and shoes, a hat that kept popping off his head, and a charming style, the young comic had shuffled his way into the public's heart. Charlie had a grace and an impishness that set him apart from other Keystone performers. He could make people laugh *and* cry.

As the months passed, Charlie acted in more and more films, including *His Favorite Pastime; Cruel, Cruel Love; The Star Boarder; Caught in a Cabaret;* and others—all made in 1914. As a result, Charlie quickly learned all about film-making. He even tried to make suggestions to Sennett for improvements, but Sennett ignored them. Although it was difficult for Sennett to admit, Charlie was outgrowing his material at Keystone.

Aware of his rising popularity, Charlie wanted to direct his own films. He refused to work with Henry Lehrman and threatened to quit Keystone. When Sennett learned that Chaplin was receiving job offers from other studios, he offered him a three-year contract and more money. But Charlie wasn't interested in three more years at Keystone. He felt it was time to move on.

In August 1914, Charlie wrote to his brother in London, telling him that he planned to leave Keystone. But he also told Sydney that he was recommending him to Sennett. Charlie hoped Sydney would come to California and negotiate his own contract to become a Keystone comic.

"Mr. Sennett is a lovely man, and we are great pals," wrote Charlie, "but business is business." At the age of twenty-five, Charlie wanted to manage his own career. He wanted to write, direct, and star in his own movies.

Stan Laurel worked with Charlie before teaming up with Oliver Hardy.

FIVE

Moving Ahead

1914–1918

Hollywood movies in the early 1900s were very different from modern films. Silent films were usually short—lasting less than half an hour. Customers paid a five- or ten-cent admission and sat on hard wooden seats. There were no refreshments, other than those the audience brought themselves. Still, people loved going to the movies.

The actors who made them laugh and cry attracted a lot of fans. Among the most popular stars of the day were slapstick comedians Buster Keaton, Harold Lloyd, and Roscoe "Fatty" Arbuckle. Charlie's friend Stan Laurel, who would later team up in comedies with Oliver Hardy, also became a silent film favorite. By the end of 1914, Charlie Chaplin had already won a number of fans for himself.

This success allowed Charlie to accept an offer made by the Essanay Film Company in Chicago, Illinois. They offered Charlie more money and greater artistic freedom than he had at Keystone. He would not be just an actor—the studio would let Charlie direct his own movies. He arrived by train from California just three days after he had signed his new contract. The comedian was anxious to get to work.

But when Charlie arrived, he found a discouraging situation. Accustomed to the sunny warmth of California, Charlie felt oppressed by the chill of Chicago in January. The Essanay studio had poor equipment and a staff who showed little concern for quality. Charlie could not understand why studio lights were turned off at 6:00 P.M. and everyone went home, even if a scene was not finished. He wanted everything to be perfect and expected everyone else to be just as dedicated as he was. He also got upset when he was given a script for his first film. Charlie explained that he wrote his own material and firmly declined the script offered to him.

Not everything at the new studio was troubling, though. Charlie was delighted to discover a comic actor at Essanay whose style blended with his own. Ben Turpin, a scrawny, cross-eyed comedian, became one of Charlie's best comedy partners. Charlie used Turpin in many of his films made at Essanay, including his first, *His New Job*. The picture, released in February 1915, did better than any previous Essanay film.

Despite his success, Charlie was not happy. He informed the studio that he could not continue working in Chicago, even though he had signed a contract. Anxious not to lose the new star, the head of Essanay transferred Charlie to a studio in Niles, California, a few miles outside of San Francisco. The Niles studio was small, but Charlie found the climate and atmosphere more comfortable.

Charlie's first film at Niles was *A Night Out*. In this picture, Charlie Chaplin and Ben Turpin play a pair of drunks who try to stand up to cops, waiters, and hostile strangers in a bar. *A Night Out* helped launch the career of a new comedy performer, Edna Purviance. By the time Charlie made *A Jitney Elopement,* his fourth film with Edna, he knew that her talent and beauty added a touch of class to his pictures.

Also in 1915, Charlie starred in *The Tramp,* playing his famous Tramp character, whom he liked to call "the little fellow." In the film, Charlie saves Edna from a gang of robbers by chasing them into a lake. When he is rewarded with a job as a hired hand on her father's farm, he does everything hilariously wrong. He accidentally drops a sack full of flour on the farmer's foot. He tries to milk a cow by pumping her tail. When the robbers attack the farmhouse, Charlie chases them with a club and is wounded by one of the fleeing crooks. He becomes a local hero and wins Edna's admiration. To his dismay, though, her boyfriend shows up. Devastated, the Tramp

Charlie naps with his feet on a customer, while Ben Turpin raises his glass in A Night Out.

packs his few things in a bandanna, squares his drooping shoulders, and walks away, twirling his skinny cane.

In *The Bank,* made in 1915, Charlie plays a janitor who spends most of his time mopping the floors of a bank. Edna, the lovely bank secretary, is the object of his affection. Though he sends her flowers, she remains unaware of his feelings. When robbers hold up the bank, Charlie chases them away and saves the grateful Edna. As they kiss, the scene fades, and Charlie wakes from a dream to find himself tenderly embracing his mop.

No matter what the plot, the Tramp managed to keep his dignity, always facing up to bullies and somehow outsmarting them. When the Tramp lost his job or his girlfriend, the audience shared his hurt. But when he straightened his bow tie, twirled his cane, and sauntered off into the sunset, they felt confident that he would survive.

Sydney Chaplin, meanwhile, had joined with Mack Sennett in Hollywood. But after his contract with Sennett expired, Sydney became Charlie's business manager. In 1916, Sydney left for New York to negotiate a new contract for his brother. A few days later, Charlie decided to take a short but much needed vacation and joined Sydney. As Charlie's train traveled toward New York, cheering crowds turned out to greet him at each stop. But the crowds upset Charlie. Although he was now one of the most famous comedians in America, he was not happy. He was shy, and he felt that the people who applauded him were not his friends. How could they know the real Charlie Chaplin?

When Charlie reached New York, several uniformed police officers escorted him off the train before he reached

This promotional poster shows Charlie's brother, Sydney, as the characters he played for Keystone.

Grand Central Station, where a huge crowd waited to glimpse their favorite star. Sydney had a limousine waiting. As they drove away, Sydney told Charlie that a company called Mutual Film Corporation had agreed to a contract of $670,000 a year, payable at $10,000 a week with a $150,000 bonus. This was an enormous salary for an actor. Charlie was stunned.

With Mutual, Charlie had complete control of all his projects. He allowed no one else to do any of the planning or writing. He trusted only his own feelings about his movies, taking advice from no one. Frequently he would wake up at dawn, work all day, and continue into the night. Because his goal was perfection, Charlie was prepared to spend all his time on his films.

In 1914, World War I had broken out in Europe. At first, only European nations were involved in the conflict. But the

United States entered the war in 1917. During the war years, Charlie Chaplin movies were in great demand around the world. Known in different countries as "Carlos," "Carlito," and "Charlot," Chaplin helped people forget the misery and suffering of war.

When U.S. troops joined the fighting, Charlie went on several tours, entertaining soldiers and helping to sell war bonds—certificates issued by the government to raise money for supplies and weapons. Some people thought that Charlie should have returned to England to fight for his own country, since he was still a British citizen. But Charlie preferred to remain in America and contribute to the war effort in his own way.

This picture from Shoulder Arms *shows the Tramp with his bathtub, cheese grater, egg beater, and potato masher.*

When he returned from his third tour, Charlie started work on a film called *Shoulder Arms.* In this movie, he plays an awkward soldier whose own feet keep getting in his way. He prepares for emergencies by attaching a blanket, a tin bathtub, a coffee pot, an egg beater, and a cheese grater to his uniform. Because he doesn't get mail from home, he looks over a buddy's shoulder and shares his letter. When a package from home finally arrives, it contains a smelly cheese. Charlie has to put on a gas mask just to unwrap it.

When a volunteer is needed for a special mission, Charlie bravely steps forward. Disguised as a tree, he wanders through enemy territory and is surprised by a German squad. Wildly swinging a huge club, he manages to dispose of the enemy. Then a Frenchwoman (played by Edna Purviance) helps the plucky soldier disguise himself as a German officer. In enemy territory, he captures the German kaiser (ruler) and the crown prince and delivers them to headquarters. As a final gesture, Charlie cannot resist aiming a hearty kick at the kaiser's backside. When his fellow soldiers start to cheer, the hero wakes up to find himself back in boot camp.

In October 1918, *Shoulder Arms* was released to the public. Charlie was concerned that some people might be offended by his comic treatment of the war. But a month later, World War I came to an end, and the country was in the mood to laugh. *Shoulder Arms* was a hit, especially with the soldiers who had just returned from the fighting.

Charlie, right, promoted U. S. savings bonds with his friends Douglas Fairbanks and Mary Pickford.

SIX

Failure and Success

1918–1921

Though Charlie continued to grow more popular with each film, his private life was far from satisfying. Many women found the comedian attractive, but he remained shy and reserved. One of the few friends he made was Douglas Fairbanks, a charming actor who was as outgoing as Charlie was shy. The two men shared a quirky sense of humor. Away from work, Charlie enjoyed spending time with Douglas and his wife, actor Mary Pickford.

One evening at a party given by Hollywood producer Samuel Goldwyn, Charlie met a pretty young girl named Mildred Harris. Her adoring gaze reminded him of Hetty Kelly, his first love. Charlie thought he might find happiness with Mildred, and just a few weeks after meeting her, he proposed. The couple married on October 23, 1918.

Charlie bought a house in North Hollywood and tried to adjust to married life, but change didn't come easy. As he had done when he was single, he left for his studio early every morning and came home late every night. Charlie's dedication to his work began to hurt his marriage. When Mildred told her husband she was expecting a baby, they both hoped that their situation would improve.

In July 1919, Mildred had a baby boy. Sadly, the child lived for only a few days. Charlie was heartbroken. But instead of turning to his wife for comfort, he became moody and withdrawn. Mildred tried, but she couldn't snap Charlie out of his misery. Charlie not only mourned the death of his child but he also realized that his marriage was a failure. In August 1920, Charlie moved out of the house and went to live in a private men's club. Soon after, Mildred filed for divorce.

Trying to forget his troubles, Charlie worked swiftly to make two new films. But neither one was successful. One day, still feeling depressed, he went to the Orpheum Theater in Los Angeles to see a musical variety show. One of the show's dancers, Jack Coogan, brought out his four-year-old son

Charlie married Mildred Harris in 1918, but the marriage lasted only a few years.

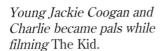

Young Jackie Coogan and Charlie became pals while filming The Kid.

Jackie. Smiling and waving as he moved gracefully around the stage, the small boy imitated his father's dance steps while the audience cheered.

Watching young Jackie, Charlie was reminded of himself in London years earlier. He was captivated by the little boy's radiant smile. For several days, Charlie thought about Jackie Coogan. He wondered whether the boy might be the right star for a new film called *The Kid.* The more Charlie thought about it, the more he felt that Jackie was the perfect actor for the title role.

Charlie went to see Jackie's parents and offered their son a part in his next film. Performers themselves, Mr. and Mrs. Coogan realized that this was a great opportunity for Jackie. Then Charlie sat down and talked to Jackie as if Charlie were a child himself. Jackie liked Charlie from the moment they met. Young Jackie was not aware of Charlie's fame. He simply enjoyed being in the older man's company. When Charlie asked Jackie what he did, the small boy serenely recited a line

Jackie and Charlie try to avoid the law in The Kid.

from his father's show, "I am a prestidigitator who works in a world of legerdemain." Charlie was charmed by the four-year-old's dexterity with words.

During filming of *The Kid,* Jackie's parents were always on the set. They were delighted to watch Jackie and Charlie develop a close friendship. Sometimes Charlie and Jackie would wander around the orange groves outside the studio. Offscreen as well as on, the comedian treated Jackie almost as if he were his own child.

The Kid took almost eighteen months to complete. The film told the story of the bond between an orphaned boy and his adopted parent. Jackie, playing the Kid, and Charlie, in his familiar role as the Tramp, made an extraordinary team.

During filming, Jackie followed Charlie's instructions with few mistakes. Some scenes were more difficult than others. But with Charlie's patient coaching and several rehearsals, Jackie made each scene perfect.

On screen, the opening title read, "A comedy with a smile—and perhaps a tear." When the film was released in 1921, audiences were so moved by the story that they often did more crying than smiling. The film became a record-breaking success and was shown in fifty countries.

After the success of *The Kid,* Charlie arranged to bring his mother to the United States. He saw to it that Hannah had a new wardrobe for the trip. He and his brother met her when she arrived in California. They hadn't seen her in nine years, and they were saddened to see how much their mother had aged. Despite her shaky mental health, Hannah was happy to settle down in a little house with a garden in Santa Monica. Charlie arranged for a nurse and housekeeper to look after his mother. Once or twice, Charlie took Hannah to the studio to show her around. But she was dazed by the bright lights and had to be taken home.

Working on a new film was always a great way for Charlie to put aside his worries. After his divorce was finalized, he spent considerable time on a picture called *The Idle Class* (1921). In this movie, Charlie played dual roles: an alcoholic socialite and the Tramp. Because Charlie had grown up poor, he liked playing the part of the poor man more than that of the rich man.

In August 1921, Charlie decided that he wanted to visit England. For some time he had been reminiscing about his first love, Hetty, and decided on a whim to look her up. What

Hannah Chaplin, Charlie's mother, visits his studio not long before her death.

he did not know was that Hetty had recently died from a sudden illness. He didn't learn of her death until he'd already arrived in London. The news came as a profound shock.

Because the British media had discovered and publicized Charlie's visit, he found thousands of fans waiting for him at Waterloo Station. At his hotel, he walked onto the balcony to wave at the cheering crowds. They yelled, "Here he is! Here he is! Good old Charlie!"

Charlie was pleasantly surprised by the warm welcome, but he wanted to get away by himself. As soon as he could, he changed his clothes, took the freight elevator downstairs, and slipped out a back entrance. A block away, he hailed a cab and went to the neighborhood where he had lived as a boy. He gazed up at the window of the tiny room where he and Sydney had looked out at the world and made up stories with their mother. He spent the afternoon revisiting other places from his childhood—even Lambeth Workhouse, its iron gates still as tall and grim as he remembered.

From London, Charlie went to Paris to attend a charity performance of *The Kid*. The French fans were just as loud and noisy as the Americans and the English. While in Paris, Charlie met the French cartoonist Cami, whom he had admired for years. The two artists had a whole conversation using only gestures—no words. "It did not occur to me that he did not speak French," the cartoonist said later. In October 1921, a weary Charlie returned to the United States.

Charlie, left, *seen here in his Tramp costume and a cape, directs*
The Gold Rush.

 SEVEN

New Horizons

1921–1930

One weekend in October 1923, when Charlie was visiting the Fairbanks's home, Douglas Fairbanks invited his friend to look at some slides. Some of the pictures showed the frozen Klondike region of Alaska. One photograph showed Chilkoot Pass, the pathway into Yukon country, where thousands of prospectors had traveled during the frantic gold rush of 1898. In the picture, a long line of prospectors struggled to climb a snow-covered mountain. A caption described the severe hardships the gold miners had suffered.

Charlie's imagination was stirred by the picture. He did some research about other cold-weather disasters. He read about the Donner party, a group that found themselves snowbound in the Sierra Nevada mountains on their way to California in 1846. Out of 160 men, women, and children, only 18 of them came through the harsh winter alive. Most died of cold and starvation. Some were forced to eat their dead comrades to survive.

Though Charlie knew he would be dealing with grim subjects, he was fascinated by the idea of a film about the Alaska gold rush. It would not be easy to film a story of the frozen north in sunny Southern California, but Charlie proceeded with excitement to make *The Gold Rush*.

For two months, Charlie prepared his studio for what he called "the Northern Story." Fur coats and hats, heavy boots, and dogsleds were imported from cold places. Charlie even asked his set designers to build a huge, snowy mountain out of 100 barrels of flour, 200 tons of plaster, and 285 tons of salt. The blizzard scenes involved four cartloads of confetti.

For one scene, Charlie hired 500 extras and took them on a train to the foot of Mount Lincoln in Summit, California. When they arrived, Charlie spoke to the extras through a megaphone, explaining that they were to hike up a narrow two-mile pass between two mountains. With cameras carefully positioned, the director gave the order to start filming. Several hundred extras struggled upward, following instructions until Charlie was satisfied and the climbers were exhausted.

As usual, the Tramp has the starring role. In one scene, the Tramp is so hungry that he boils his shoe and eats it, picking out the nails as though they are bones and twirling the shoelaces as though they are strands of spaghetti. Charlie made the scene realistic by using special shoes made out of licorice. In the same scene, Charlie's companion, Big Jim, is so hungry that he imagines Charlie has turned into a chicken. Dressed in feathers, Charlie scrambles around a cabin squawking and flapping his arms as Big Jim chases after him with a knife.

Balancing humor with sentiment, the movie also included some sad moments. In one scene, the Tramp is alone on New

Year's Eve. Though he has prepared a festive meal for two pretty dance-hall hostesses, they fail to show up. Waiting patiently, he admires the tablecloth he has made out of his shirt. He folds the sleeves artistically to make them look like elegant dinner napkins. When Charlie finally realizes the women have

Charlie, lower left, *is dwarfed by the mountains in a mining camp scene from* The Gold Rush.

forgotten all about him, he heaves a sigh and rubs his eyes. He shuffles sadly through the snow to the dance hall. Looking through the window, he sees the women having a good time inside. Once again, the Tramp is alone. However, the film ends happily when Charlie finds true love and a huge pile of gold.

On August 16, 1925, *The Gold Rush* opened at the Strand Theater in New York and met with great fanfare. The public

With wife Lita Grey, Charlie had two children, Charles Jr., left, and Sydney.

and the critics extended enthusiastic praise for the star as well as the picture. One American critic called Chaplin "a mythical hero, now a figure of poetry, now a type out of the funny papers." A British critic wrote, *"The Gold Rush* is the funniest film I have ever seen. It is probably the funniest film that anyone has ever seen." The movie brought in record earnings of $6 million.

Charlie could plan happy endings for his films, but he was unable to do the same in real life. During the filming of *The Gold Rush,* he fell in love with a sixteen-year-old performer, Lita Grey, who played a dance-hall girl in the movie. Lita's mother was not pleased when she discovered that her teenage daughter was secretly dating the thirty-five-year-old comedian. Charlie tried to convince the woman that he intended to marry Lita, but she still disapproved of the relationship. Upon learning that her daughter was pregnant, Lita's mother changed her mind.

On November 24, 1924, Charlie and Lita were married. Despite having two children together—Charles Jr. and Sydney Earle—Charlie and Lita proved to be incompatible, and the marriage lasted just a few years. In 1927, the couple was divorced.

While Charlie's divorce case was pending, he began work on another film—*The Circus.* In this movie, the Tramp becomes caught up in the hectic world of a traveling circus. Chased into the circus ring by the police, he unintentionally triggers roars of laughter from the spectators. Seeing this, the circus owner gives Charlie a job as a clown. Charlie falls in love with the circus owner's beautiful stepdaughter. He hopes his love will be returned. But when a handsome new performer, Rex the High Wire Walker, arrives on the scene, the clown realizes he is out of luck. Before giving up completely,

Charlie is in trouble on the high wire in The Circus.

he decides to compete with his rival by trying to walk the tightrope with comedic success.

To prepare for the scene, Charlie learned to balance and walk on a tightrope in just one week. At first, the rope was stretched only a foot off of the floor, then gradually raised closer to the ceiling. A net was placed under the tightrope, but Charlie never fell.

In another sequence, Charlie tries to prove his bravery by entering a lion's cage. Since the scene used live animals, Charlie did not have to pretend to be frightened! After more than two hundred takes, the sequence was finally completed.

Reviews of *The Circus* were nearly as enthusiastic as those for *The Gold Rush*. The film won a special Academy Award in 1928 for "versatility and genius in writing, acting, directing and producing."

In August 1928, Charlie's mother had a severe gallbladder attack. At Glendale Hospital, Charlie sat by Hannah's bedside and tried to assure her that she would soon recover. But the next day, the hospital called to inform Charlie that his mother had died. Charlie deeply mourned the loss of the courageous woman who had nurtured his artistic talent.

Grieving from the bitter events of divorce and death, Charlie once again turned to his filmmaking—the remedy that always seemed to work best. This time, however, he came up against something new. In 1930, sound movies—called "talkies"—arrived in Hollywood. Up until that time, Charlie's success had come from his natural gift for pantomime. If he tried to speak in the movies, would talking destroy his unique characters such as the Tramp? Charlie was determined to find out.

This actor is learning to perfect her voice for the new "talking pictures."

EIGHT

Citizen of the World

1930–1936

On July 8, 1928, Warner Brothers film company pro-
duced *Lights of New York,* the first talking film to come out of
Hollywood. In another popular talkie, *The Jazz Singer* starring
Al Jolson, the actors both talked and sang.

Charlie was puzzled and unhappy about the favorable publicity these films received. It appeared as if talkies might become all the rage. But Charlie did not believe that sound
movies were as effective as silent films. The physical gestures
and facial expressions of the Tramp could be understood by
people all over the world—no matter what language they
spoke. Charlie did not want to see the talking films undermine
the power of pantomime.

Determined to make another silent film, Charlie concen-
trated on a picture called *City Lights.* This movie was set in a
mythical city that combined the cosmopolitan atmospheres of
London, Paris, and Naples. *City Lights* tells the story of a blind
woman who is a flower vendor and who believes that her kind

customer—the Tramp—is a millionaire. The Tramp is touched by her plight and is determined to find the money for an operation to restore her sight. Once the blind girl can see, however, the Tramp is too shy to let her know that he is the one who has helped her.

For this film, Charlie added something new. Though he had never written music before, he enlisted the help of a professional music arranger to help him create an original composition for the film. He was thrilled to hear his own tunes played for the first time by a large orchestra. After using music in *City Lights,* Charlie continued to include it in all his pictures.

When a sneak preview of *City Lights* ran in Los Angeles, the response was not very enthusiastic. The audience was mostly local theatergoers. They were expecting a movie more in the style of the new talking pictures, something more realistic and unique. A few people even walked out of the theater before the film was over. But when the movie premiered two weeks later, the film's publicity had done its job. Viewers were looking forward to something more nostalgic, and movie stars packed the Los Angeles theater.

In February 1931, *City Lights* ran from 9:00 A.M. until midnight at the George M. Cohan Theater, where it had opened in New York. Mobs of patrons gathered outside the theater early in the morning and all through the day to see the movie. *City Lights* was hailed as a masterpiece. Film critic Alexander Woollcott commented, "[Chaplin's] like has not passed this way before. And we shall not see his like again." Producer and screenwriter Jerry Epstein, who worked with Chaplin several years later, wrote, "After the film I couldn't sleep. It was like beholding Michelangelo's *David* for the first time. I walked along Hollywood Boulevard all night in a daze, feeling melancholy, exhilarated, but above all thrilled that I

Virginia Cherrill, playing the blind flower girl in City Lights, *puts a flower in Charlie's lapel.*

knew the creator of this masterpiece." Within twelve weeks, *City Lights* had grossed $400,000, making it Chaplin's most successful production to date.

In London for the European premiere of *City Lights,* Charlie was again met by enthusiastic crowds. From his hotel window, he noticed that several people held up signs. One read, "Charlie is still our darling."

Nonstop work had exhausted Charlie physically and mentally, so he stayed in Europe for a vacation. During his stay, he met many celebrities, including British prime minister Lloyd George, playwright George Bernard Shaw, writer H. G. Wells, and Indian spiritual and political leader Mohandas Gandhi (who had never seen a Chaplin film). Though he enjoyed the

Charlie was introduced to Indian leader Mohandas Gandhi while vacationing in Europe.

hobnobbing, Charlie managed to take time to visit the Hanwell School, where he had lived as a small boy. Hanwell was still an orphanage, but it seemed to have many more occupants than Charlie remembered.

When the children at Hanwell learned that Charlie Chaplin was coming, they were wild with excitement. As the film star entered the dining hall, four hundred youngsters yelled and cheered until they were hoarse. Charlie entertained them with a spontaneous program of impersonations and pantomime, twirling his cane and shuffling around the room. Recalling the miserable Christmas at Hanwell, when he had been punished for forgetting to make his bed, Charlie sent gifts of candy, fruit, and toys to all the children. He also promised them that he would send a movie projector so they could see all of his movies.

After London, Charlie continued on to Paris, Vienna, and Berlin. In Germany, crowds lined the route from the railway station to the hotel. Charlie was entertained by members of the German government and given a guided tour of Berlin.

The next morning, however, the German media reacted angrily. The National Socialist Party—better known as the Nazis—was gaining power in Germany. The Nazis were stirring up hatred against Jews, and after Chaplin's visit, some writers scolded the people of Berlin for applauding "a Jewish comedian from America." No one had bothered to find out that Charlie's parents were Gentiles of Irish and French descent. The Nazis instead assumed that Charlie was Jewish. The comedian made no attempt to correct the assumption. He commented, "I'm a logical choice. I look the part, I'm a Jew, and I'm a comedian."

After Berlin, Charlie traveled to France to visit his brother, who had retired in the town of Nice. Charlie's vacation was prolonged when Douglas Fairbanks invited the brothers to his home in Saint-Moritz, Switzerland. From Switzerland, Charlie and Sydney decided to go to the Far East. They visited Singapore, Ceylon (modern-day Sri Lanka), Bali, and Japan.

Charlie was fascinated by Japanese culture, particularly its tea ceremonies and wood-block art. He loved the Kabuki—a two-hundred-year-old form of musical theater. Japanese crowds welcomed Charlie as enthusiastically as crowds all over Europe.

When their trip was over, Sydney returned to Nice and Charlie left for home by boat. During the voyage across the Atlantic, he started thinking about a new film. For more than a year, some critics had been calling his work out of date—especially compared to the talkies. Charlie decided that his next film would focus on current events. But it would still be silent, except for sound effects and musical accompaniment.

When he returned to the United States, Charlie found the country suffering from an economic crisis that came to be known as the Great Depression. Following the disastrous stock market crash of 1929, millions of people lost their jobs, and many lost their homes as well. To make matters worse, a severe drought in the Great Plains ruined crops and killed livestock. Thousands of farmers were forced to abandon their farms and seek jobs elsewhere.

Trying to escape their despair, Americans turned to film comedies, especially Charlie's. Laughter brought relief to their grim lives. Because of his own childhood poverty, Charlie understood the country's suffering. He particularly sympathized with ordinary working people.

For years, Charlie had been talking about making a movie that, in a comic way, criticized the problems of the factory system. In 1921 he had visited a Ford automobile assembly plant in Detroit. Looking down at the assembly line from a catwalk, or suspended walkway, Charlie was struck by the dull, mechanical, repetitive work taking place below. He decided that his next film would address his concerns about the plight of factory workers.

Charlie's new picture, *Modern Times,* took ten months to complete. Though the film contained numerous funny scenes, the underlying message was serious. Charlie wanted to show the darker side of a society that valued money above human dignity. In the opening scene, the camera follows a flock of sheep pushing through a stockyard gate, moving ahead blindly. The scene changes to a crowd of factory workers shoving their way into a factory yard. The camera zeros in on Charlie, a harried factory worker. He is forced to move faster and faster as his boss speeds up the machinery. Charlie tries to control the machines, but they get away from him and self-destruct. In a frenzy, Charlie pulls the plant's control levers, grabs an oil can, and squirts everyone in sight, including the boss.

After Charlie recovers from this mishap, he walks the streets looking for employment. He meets a homeless young orphan played by Paulette Goddard. She helps him get a job as a singing waiter in a café. For the first time in a movie, Charlie sings in a clear, melodious voice. His song, however, is composed of nonsense syllables. The Tramp's only true language is pantomime.

When the police come looking for Paulette, who has escaped from an orphanage, she and Charlie make their getaway together. The last scene ends on a happy note as the two walk arm in arm down a dusty road into the sunset.

The Tramp goes crazy in this scene from Modern Times.

Modern Times opened in February 1936 to mixed re-actions. While most audiences laughed and cheered, some critics were disappointed. "Went to see Charlie's picture last night," wrote author Upton Sinclair. "The part about the factory was very interesting and charming, but the rest just repeats Charlie's old material." Russian filmmaker Boris Shumiatski discussed the film's political message, noting that *Modern Times* revealed "honestly and truthfully how the American working class is carrying on the struggle against capitalism [the American industrial system]."

During filming, Paulette Goddard and Charlie had started dating. They discovered that they had many things in common. Like Charlie, Paulette had gone to work at an early age to help support her family. Both of them had endured loneliness and hunger, but their sad experiences had not prevented them from pursuing their dreams. Paulette was also serious about her acting career. Though at age forty-three, Charlie was twenty-one years older than Paulette, the age difference didn't

Charlie secretly married Paulette Goddard while traveling in Asia in 1936.

seem to affect their relationship. Paulette was warm, outgoing, and intelligent, with a delightful sense of humor.

When Charlie's two young sons met their father's new girlfriend, they adored her immediately. Paulette's youthful energy and silliness made her seem like an older sister. Paulette loved spending time with Charlie Jr. and Sydney Earle, sometimes acting as a peacemaker when the boys had a disagreement with their father. Paulette encouraged Charlie to become more involved with his sons. Together, the group attended picnics, skating parties, and outings.

Soon after *Modern Times* was finished, Charlie and Paulette took a trip to the Far East. The couple married in China without fanfare or publicity. On their return to California, the Chaplins settled into a house in Beverly Hills and continued their film careers.

Paulette wanted to audition for the part of Scarlett O'Hara in *Gone With the Wind,* but Charlie did not like the idea. Charlie was now an independent producer, and Paulette was under contract with his Chaplin Studios. Charlie did not want her to work for someone else. Nonetheless, in 1938, Paulette made two screen tests for the Scarlett role. Though the film's producers liked one test, the part was given to another actor, Vivien Leigh.

Aware of his wife's deep disappointment, Charlie tried to write a new script just for her. But his thoughts were now absorbed by a completely different project.

Vienna, Austria, was the scene of this real-life Nazi march in 1938.

More Challenges

1936–1947

In the 1930s, a dangerous dictator named Adolf Hitler had gained complete control of the German government. His political party—the Nazis—aimed to rid the world of people who did not conform to their rigid standards of "ethnic purity." In racist, hate-filled speeches, Hitler called Germans to join him in ridding their country of all groups that he deemed "inferior." These groups included Jews, Gypsies, homosexuals, and others. Hitler wanted to spread his ideas throughout Europe, and in 1938 he began a systematic invasion of neighboring European countries, beginning with Austria. Another world war seemed inevitable.

In 1938, a friend gave Charlie a small book of Nazi propaganda that criticized the so-called inferior people. Charlie was surprised to see a picture of himself in the pamphlet with a caption that read, "The little Jewish tumbler, as disgusting as he is boring."

Charlie's reaction was immediate. He believed that the best way to get revenge was to make people laugh at Hitler. At the same time, he wanted to warn people of the terrible danger the German leader posed.

Several years earlier, one of Charlie's friends had suggested he make a film mocking Hitler, but Charlie had not been ready to consider it. Now he was. Strangely enough, there was some physical resemblance between Charlie and Adolf Hitler. By adding a dark toothbrush mustache, bristling eyebrows, and exaggerated gestures, it was easy for Charlie to mimic Hitler.

Filming for *The Great Dictator* began on September 9, 1939, just one week after Hitler invaded Poland, which marked the start of World War II. In this film, Chaplin ridiculed Hitler in dual roles. One was a crude imitation of Hitler—a dictator named Adenoid Hynkel. Charlie's other character was a Jewish barber who is Hynkel's double.

As Adenoid Hynkel in The Great Dictator, *left,* Charlie looked a lot like Nazi leader Adolf Hitler, *right.*

The Great Dictator combined both pantomime and dialogue. In this film, for the first time on-screen, Charlie would speak—in two different voices. As the barber, he would utter only timid monosyllables. As the dictator, he would shout in German-sounding gibberish, accompanied by poses and wild ranting that mimicked Hitler. Charlie carefully studied and analyzed every picture and film of Adolf Hitler he could find to create the most authentic parody possible. At considerable expense, he also hired several well-known actors from outside his own studio, including Jack Oakie, Reginald Gardiner, Henry Daniell, and Billy Gilbert.

In November 1939, while Charlie was filming, he received a surprise visit from his close friend Douglas Fairbanks. Charlie put on his Hynkel costume to amuse Douglas, and they had a few laughs together. Afterward, the two men had lunch and talked about old times. But the next month, on the morning of December 12, Douglas Fairbanks's son phoned to tell Charlie that Fairbanks had died in his sleep. On the day of the funeral, the Chaplin studio canceled all filming.

Though *The Great Dictator* had many funny scenes, Charlie did not miss the chance to deliver a serious message to the world. "Now," the barber says at one point, "let us fight to free the world, to do away with national barriers, to do away with greed, with hate and intolerance. Let us fight for a world of reason—a world where science and progress will lead to all men's happiness. Soldiers, in the name of democracy, let us unite!"

The film opened at the Astor and Capitol Theaters in New York on October 15, 1940. Reviews were mixed. The *New York Herald-Tribune* declared, *"The Great Dictator* is aflame with Chaplin's genius but the flame flickers badly." The British, who were under German air attack at the time, loved the parody of

Hitler. A critic in Britain's *New Statesman* and *Nation* called the movie "the best heartener we have, with war standing still or going for or against us." Overall, the film was a success and earned more money than any previous Chaplin picture.

That year, Charlie received a Best Actor award from the New York Film Critic's Circle for his performance in *The Great Dictator.* But Charlie refused to accept the award. He felt that his picture deserved an award, not his acting, and was insulted that the film itself had been ignored. Charlie's publicity manager, Albert Margolies, noted that "Many hurtful things happened to Chaplin all through his life, many more than he deserved. But I doubt whether any caused him more pain than to be regarded as a mere actor."

Though Paulette Goddard had an important role as Hannah (Hynkel's girlfriend) in *The Great Dictator,* her contract with Chaplin Studios was almost expired. Charlie was furious when Paulette asked to be released from her obligations with his company so that she could sign on with another studio. She meant no disloyalty to Charlie, but she was a talented actor, and she wanted to move on with her career. The disagreement between the couple began to affect their marriage.

In 1941, Japan—Germany's ally—attacked a U.S. naval base in Pearl Harbor, Hawaii. With this attack, the United States entered World War II. Charlie took a deep interest in the war. When Hitler attacked Russia, Charlie made several speeches urging Americans to contribute funds for Russian war relief.

Although Russia and the United States were allies during World War II, Russia was a communist country. Many Americans didn't like the communist political system, which called

U.S. General Eisenhower, front left, *encourages American troops during World War II.*

for an end to private business ownership. Charlie's political activity on behalf of Russia was viewed with suspicion in the United States. Several newspaper columnists attacked Charlie, saying that he preferred Communism. Other journalists noted that although Charlie had lived in the United States for many years, he had never become an American citizen.

In response to these attacks, Charlie insisted he was not a communist. He sympathized with the Russian people in their wartime suffering. As for his citizenship, Charlie said that while he was glad to be living in the United States, he considered himself a citizen of the world.

In 1942, Charlie's third marriage ended after six years. He had no sooner finalized the divorce when other problems arose. A young actor named Joan Barry claimed that Charlie

When Oona O'Neill married Charlie, she broke her father's heart.

Chaplin was the father of her child. She promised not to press charges if he gave her a large sum of money.

Though he admitted to having had a relationship with Joan, Charlie protested that he was not the child's father. He claimed that the young woman was mentally unstable, and he refused to be blackmailed. After three years and two trials, neither jury could reach a unanimous verdict. Finally, the judge ruled that Charlie had to pay child support anyway.

While Charlie was going through this troubling period, something more positive happened. In the spring of 1943, Charlie was introduced to seventeen-year-old Oona O'Neill, daughter of the famous playwright Eugene O'Neill. Charlie was instantly attracted to Oona's gentle serene beauty.

Despite O'Neill's objection to his daughter's fifty-three-year-old suitor, Oona and Charlie fell deeply in love. The large difference in their ages did not matter to them. Charlie waited impatiently for Oona to reach her eighteenth birthday, when she would not need her father's consent to marry. On June 16, 1943, Oona and Charlie were married. Their first child, Geraldine, was born in August 1944.

To escape the harsh publicity that followed Joan Barry's court case against Charlie, the Chaplins went to live in the small town of Nyack, New York. Charlie thought the quiet atmosphere would help him concentrate on a new script, but he missed his California studio.

Meanwhile, Charlie's friend—actor and filmmaker Orson Welles—told him the story of a Frenchman who allegedly murdered his many wives for their money. Though the subject was grim, Charlie thought the story had potential as a dark comedy. Charlie turned the idea into a film called *Monsieur Verdoux,* the story of a bank clerk who goes about his dull job until the depression of the 1930s makes him desperate. Verdoux resorts to marrying wealthy women and murdering them for their money.

The Chaplins returned to Beverly Hills and Charlie went to work on his new script. It took two years to finish the writing. But the film was shot in twelve weeks, a record for Charlie.

With this film, for the first time in his movie career, Charlie abandoned his famous Tramp character and took on a more serious role. As Verdoux, he played a well-dressed, middle-class businessman who becomes so frustrated by economic and social problems that he is forced to murder to survive.

When critics viewed *Monsieur Verdoux* on April 11, 1947, their reactions were mostly negative. Some came away upset and disappointed by the film's morbid theme. Others felt cheated out of the lighthearted laughter they associated with Charlie's films. The American public, not accustomed to dark comedy—

especially from an actor like Charlie Chaplin—seemed to feel the same way. The film had a short New York run. Several states even banned *Monsieur Verdoux* on the grounds that "it made a joke of murder or that its maker was not a very nice man." In some cities, protesters who were still upset about Charlie's wartime politics picketed movie theaters until they stopped showing the film.

In parts of Europe, however, the picture received more favorable notices, even winning a few awards. Only one critic in the United States, the writer James Agee, enjoyed *Monsieur Verdoux,* calling it Charlie's most fascinating picture and "high among the great works of this century." But one good review was not enough for Charlie. He had the film withdrawn from distribution in the United States.

Charlie, as Monsieur Verdoux, listens to a seashell.

On April 12, 1947, the day after *Monsieur Verdoux* opened, Charlie agreed to hold a press conference in New York to try to put an end to the controversy about the film. At the conference, Charlie was questioned rudely by reporters about his patriotism and his political connections. Quietly defending himself, the comedian explained that his loyalty was not confined to any one country, but to the entire world and all people—even those who found him objectionable.

Shortly after the press conference, Charlie learned that the House Un-American Activities Committee (HUAC) was planning to question him about his alleged communist beliefs. HUAC, a congressional committee, had begun to investigate prominent Americans suspected of communist activities. Some committee members were convinced that communists had taken over the film industry.

Charlie's appearance before the committee was postponed many times. He finally wrote a letter to the committee stating that he had never been a member of the communist party. He defended his loyalty and his work during the war. He further explained, as he had previously to reporters, that he considered himself to be a citizen of the whole world. The committee thanked him for the information, also by letter. Charlie thought the matter was finished.

Joseph McCarthy, right, *made it his mission to try to root out communism in the United States.*

TEN

Exile

1947–1956

In the late 1940s, a U.S. senator named Joseph McCarthy had stepped up the anticommunist campaign in Congress. Among the suspected communists were a number of people in the film and theater industries. Charlie made no attempt to conceal his friendship with many of these people, including the playwright Bertolt Brecht and the singer Paul Robeson.

In an atmosphere of growing mistrust and suspicion, Charlie refused to be intimidated. When, in April 1948, the Federal Bureau of Investigation (FBI) questioned him closely about his personal life and political beliefs, he responded by saying he was decidedly liberal and did not hate communists.

Despite the pressure of the political investigation, Charlie immersed himself in the planning and writing of a new film. By 1952, he had devoted more than three years to the project, eventually calling it *Limelight*. The story of an aging music hall performer and the girl he helps to achieve stardom is romantic and sentimental. Charlie incorporated into the film his memories of the theater and of his early life in London. Since the main character was an aging actor facing failure and the destructive power of alcohol, some people believed that *Limelight* was based on Charlie's father's life.

Charlie cast his own children in several of the film's sequences. Oona and Charlie's first daughter, Geraldine, had been followed by Michael in 1946, Josephine in 1949, and Victoria in 1951. Charlie assigned parts to every child who could walk and talk. For the young lead, Neville, he cast his son Sydney, then age twenty-six. Charles Jr. had a small role as a clown, and Geraldine, Michael, and Josephine appeared briefly as street urchins in the opening scene.

Limelight was to premiere in London. Charlie and Oona decided to take the family there for the event and enjoy a vacation together afterward. Oona had never been to England and looked forward to the trip.

On September 17, 1952, the Chaplins and their four children sailed for Europe on the SS *Queen Elizabeth*. Two days later, while the family was still at sea, U.S. Attorney General James McGranery notified Charlie that he was barred from returning to the United States on the grounds of communist affiliation.

Charlie and Oona were stunned. For forty years Charlie had made the United States his home. Now he was forbidden to return to the land he had come to love more than his birthplace. Charlie and Oona were forced to prepare their children to face an unknown future in exile.

When news of the ruling reached the American press, reactions were fast and furious. A Hollywood columnist named Hedda Hopper claimed that though Charlie was a good actor, he was in fact anti-American and had no right "to go against our customs, to abhor everything we stand for, to throw our hospitality back in our faces.... Good riddance to bad company." William Bradford Huie, editor of the *American Mercury,* said that Charlie loved no one but himself and loathed the poor.

Charlie did have defenders, however. Editorials appeared in the *Nation* and the *New York Times* that supported Charlie. Actor Mary Pickford said that the action of the attorney general and the United States was undignified. Comedian Buster Keaton pointed out that in the twenty-five years he had known Charlie, he never once heard him utter a political opinion.

When Charlie arrived in London, the crowds were not as large as they had been on his previous visits, but eager fans still broke through the police barriers to touch him. Charlie felt gratified to see a pile of fan letters waiting for him at his hotel. Many of them asked him to remain in England. The British public was enchanted by Oona and the children.

Many U. S. theaters refused to show the movie Limelight *because of talk that Charlie was a communist sympathizer.*

For *Limelight's* world premiere in London, many British celebrities were in attendance, including Princess Margaret. Moving on to Paris for the French opening, the Chaplins were invited to lunch with the French president, and Charlie was made an officer of the Legion of Honor.

But back in the United States, the American Legion and other veterans' groups boycotted the showing of *Limelight,* convinced that Charlie was a threat to the United States. Large theater chains were persuaded to withdraw the movie after its premiere. When Oona flew back to California to take care of the family's affairs, she discovered that the FBI had questioned the family's servants about the Chaplins. Agents had contacted anyone who had ever known Charlie, hoping to uncover something that would incriminate him. Lita Grey, Charlie's second wife, was questioned. But she refused to divulge any details of their life together.

A few days after Oona returned from California, the Chaplins packed and left for Switzerland, where they had decided to make their home. In January 1953, in the village of Corsier-sur-Vevey, they bought a spacious villa, Manoir de Ban, that had formerly belonged to an American ambassador. Surrounded by thirty-seven acres of orchards and gardens, the house had three floors and eighteen rooms. On the third floor, the children and their nannies had plenty of space. (The four children born in the United States were eventually joined by four sisters and brothers: Eugene in 1953, Jane in 1958, Annette in 1960, and Christopher in 1962.)

When Charlie wanted quiet, he retired to the library on the ground floor. He also built a special air-conditioned room in the cellar to store his scripts, business records, and photographs. In a studio on the second floor, Oona devoted herself to painting, which had always been a favorite endeavor of hers.

While in exile, the Chaplins lived in this house in Switzerland.

The large staff of seventeen servants, including gardeners and a chauffeur, functioned smoothly under Oona's guidance. Charlie was delighted when the gardeners were able to grow all the family's vegetables, including his favorite—fresh corn on the cob. Although the Chaplins avoided large parties and receptions, after a while they became part of the community, shopping in town and attending local events.

Once Charlie was comfortably settled in Switzerland, he sold his studio and house in Beverly Hills but received substantially less than the asking price for both. A short time later, to show support for her husband, Oona Chaplin renounced her American citizenship.

For about six months, Charlie enjoyed the peace and quiet of his Swiss retreat. But he was not the kind of person

*Charlie and Oona had
seven children together.
Left to right: Eugene,
Charlie holding Jane,
Geraldine, Michael,
Josephine, Oona holding
Annette, and Victoria.*

to remain inactive for very long. By the end of 1953, he started
to plan his eightieth screen production, *The King in New York.*
He worked on the script for the next year and a half. In the
fall of 1955, it was ready for production. With the help of Jerry
Epstein, the assistant producer on *Limelight,* Charlie estab-
lished a new production company, Attica, and rented studio
facilities in London.

Charlie planned to play the lead role of an exiled king
who arrives in New York full of optimism and plans to pro-
mote world peace. Unfortunately, the king gets involved in a
political "witch hunt," similar to the ordeal that Charlie had
been through with HUAC and Senator McCarthy. In the film,
the king befriends a young boy whose parents have been accused of communism in the witch hunt.

Charlie searched for a young actor to play the part of the
boy, then finally cast his own son Michael. Oona and Charlie

thought that perhaps their son should change his name for the part so Charlie would not be accused of favoritism. But Michael insisted on using his given name.

Producing *The King in New York* was stressful for Charlie. Used to running his own film company, he now had to work in a rented studio with only one familiar associate, Jerry Epstein.

Though there were some fine moments in *The King in New York,* it was not a commercial success. The British press gave it generally favorable reviews, calling it better than most Hollywood films. Ever the perfectionist, Charlie himself was disappointed. Years later he admitted that the film was some- what "heavy-handed."

On April 16, 1956, Charlie's brother died in Nice. After Sydney's retirement, the two brothers had grown closer. They especially enjoyed getting together for reunions and trips whenever they could. In their youth, Sydney had always been there for his younger brother, sharing his hopes and fears, giving him guidance, financial support, and encouragement. Charlie would miss his big brother for the rest of his life.

Not everyone at Oxford University thought Charlie should be awarded an honorary degree.

ELEVEN

Sir Charles Chaplin

1956–1977

After his brother's death, Charlie thought of writing an autobiography. In 1960, he finally began to work on the book. Discipline had always come easily to Charlie. Now he settled into a daily routine of writing after breakfast and again after lunch. In fair weather, after a game of tennis, a brief nap, and dinner, Charlie would resume working in the library until bedtime. When word got out that Chaplin was writing the story of his life, offers of publication came from the United States, England, and several other European countries. But Charlie would have yet more achievements to write about.

On June 27, 1962, Charlie Chaplin received the honorary degree of Doctor of Letters from Oxford University in England. One Oxford historian publicly objected to the university giving the award to a comedian. He stated that Oxford might as well honor a clown in the circus. Dressed in academic robes of scarlet and gray, Charlie ignored the historian and rose to make a gracious acceptance speech.

"Beauty is in the eye of the beholder," said Charlie. "There are those who can see either art or beauty in a rose lying in the gutter, or the sudden slant of sunlight across an ash can, or even in the antics of a clown."

Nine days later, Charlie Chaplin was awarded another honorary degree, from the University of Durham in England. This time there were no objections, only the welcome sound of hearty applause.

As Charlie neared his seventy-fifth birthday, his memoirs reached their final stage. In September 1964, *My Autobiography* was published in a first edition of 80,000 copies. The book was soon translated into German and Italian. One American critic, Budd Schulberg, did not care for the autobiography and commented, "After all, Charlie is not a writer, but he is our only genius of the motion picture. Do you expect a butterfly to sing?" However, the book's warm reception around most of the world motivated Charlie to start work on one more picture.

At seventy-six years old, Charlie had not lost any of his creative energy. On a trip to London, he had seen actor Sophia Loren in a romantic film that intrigued him. On his return, he started to write a script about a beautiful countess who stows away in the cabin of an American diplomat on a ship leaving Hong Kong.

When he offered the female lead to Loren, she accepted without a moment's hesitation. She had always wanted to work for Charlie Chaplin. The actor Marlon Brando accepted the role of the diplomat soon afterward. In January 1966, shooting for *A Countess from Hong Kong* got under way and was completed five months later.

Even though Charlie had cast two major stars in the leading roles, the picture received poor notices. It was Charlie's first color film, but bright color and handsome performers were not enough to redeem the boring plot and somewhat dull dialogue.

Charlie pretended to be unaffected by the unfavorable reviews, but he was deeply upset. He felt that the British critics did not understand romantic comedy and had attacked him without reason. When *A Countess from Hong Kong* opened in Paris and Italy, Charlie was happy to hear it called "charming" and "funny."

On March 20, 1968, Charlie suffered one of the most painful losses of his life. His son Charlie Jr. died of a heart attack at age forty-three. Young Charlie had always wanted to be recognized as an actor on his own merits, but his famous

Charlie, seen here only as a shadow, left, *directs Sophia Loren in a rehearsal of* A Countess from Hong Kong.

When Charlie arrived in New York in 1972, it had been nearly twenty years since he had set foot in the United States.

name had been a serious obstacle. Although Charlie was grief stricken over his son's death, he again immersed himself in writing new scripts, although he would not produce any more films.

In 1971 at the Cannes Film Festival, Charlie received a special award for his work. He was also given the rank of Commander of the Legion of Honor at the festival. Meanwhile, the Academy of Motion Picture Arts and Sciences (the organization that awards Oscars) and the Lincoln Center Film Society extended a joint invitation to Charlie to visit the United States. At first Charlie was hesitant about returning to the country from which he had been exiled, although the court ruling that barred him from the United States had long since lapsed. Then, remembering that Los Angeles was the place where he had met Oona, he decided to go.

On April 2, 1972, Charlie and Oona Chaplin arrived at Kennedy Airport in New York, where they were greeted by a large crowd of photographers and journalists. As Charlie descended from the plane he blew kisses, then was whisked away to his hotel by limousine.

The next evening, the Chaplins went to Lincoln Center for a gala performance in Charlie's honor. Fifteen hundred people paid admission prices of $10 and $25. Those who attended the champagne reception afterward paid $100 and $250 each. Before the reception, the audience watched a screening of *The Kid.* When Charlie entered the hall, the audience rose and gave the actor a resounding ovation. The applause went on and on until Charlie and most of the spectators were close to tears. When the Chaplins left, police had to protect them from the surging crowd. Charlie was thrilled that he had not been forgotten. The next day, New York mayor John Lindsay presented Charlie with the Handel Medallion, New York's highest cultural award.

A few days later, the Chaplins flew to Hollywood. The reception for Charlie by the Academy of Motion Picture Arts and Sciences was even more moving than the one in New York. Charlie realized he needn't have been nervous about how people would react. He told a reporter, Bosley Crowther of the *New York Times,* "I cannot help but be bitter about many things that happened to me, but the country and the American people—they are great, of course." As he received his special Oscar, Charlie could not suppress his tears. In appreciation of his wonderful welcome, he managed to execute one of his famous Tramp gestures, making his hat spring up from his head as he had in so many films.

Charlie received a special Academy Award on his birthday in 1972.

Charlie continued to receive honors in the 1970s. At the Venice Film Festival in 1972, he was presented with a special award called the Golden Lion. Venice's St. Mark's Square was brilliantly lit and converted into an enormous open-air cinema for a showing of *City Lights.*

At the start of the screening, Charlie appeared on a balcony overlooking the square. As the crowds below broke into wild cheering and applause, the wife of the president of Italy gave Charlie his award. When the crowd finally allowed Charlie to stop waving and smiling, he was happy but tired.

Oona suggested that they should leave, but Charlie insisted on staying until he had seen his favorite part of the film—the fight sequence. With audience attention riveted on the screen, the Chaplins were able to slip quietly away without notice.

On his return home to Switzerland, Charlie began working on a special book called *My Life in Pictures.* The book, an addition to Charlie's autobiography, included a collection of private photographs never seen by the public. When he went to London to publicize the new book, Charlie told reporters he would never be able to retire because ideas were constantly popping into his head.

On January 2, 1975, Charlie went to London for what was undoubtedly the outstanding public highlight of his life. He was knighted by Queen Elizabeth II of England. As the guests

Charlie wears his ribbon and insignia after being knighted.

waited for the queen to arrive, a string orchestra played the theme music from *Limelight* and *A Countess from Hong Kong.*

Charlie was almost eighty-six years old, and his legs were too frail to walk the ten yards to reach Queen Elizabeth. A palace steward escorted the performer in a wheelchair, as Charlie's family witnessed the knighting ceremony of Sir Charles Spencer Chaplin.

Afterward, the family celebrated at the Savoy Hotel in London. In the midst of the party, Prime Minister Harold Wilson arrived to extend his personal congratulations to Sir Charles Chaplin. Thrilled at this unexpected honor, Charlie rose to his feet, responding with the energy he had always been known for. For the moment, the wheelchair was thrust out of sight and forgotten.

Over the next two years, Charlie and Oona lived quietly, rarely leaving home. Troubled by a severe case of gout (painful condition of the joints, usually of the feet), he did little walking. He spent many hours rereading his favorite Charles Dickens novel, *Oliver Twist,* and watching his old films on his home projector. When the children were small, he had not allowed them to watch television, but now he and Oona watched news programs and American films together. In good weather, the chauffeur drove them to a nearby lake where they would sit and enjoy the view. In 1976, when Charlie learned that *The King in New York* had finally been released in the United States, he was delighted.

In the fall of 1977, Charlie started to suffer from fatigue and had to remain in bed for increasing periods of time. Oona stayed with him as much as possible, but finally a nurse was hired to help with Charlie's care. At Christmas, the Chaplin children and grandchildren arrived in Switzerland to celebrate the holiday. On Christmas Eve, Charlie's bedroom door was left open so he could hear and see the family around the Christmas tree. Sometime that night, Charlie died peacefully in his sleep.

On December 27, 1977, a funeral service was held at the Anglican church in Vevey, Switzerland. In accordance with Charlie's wishes, the service was a simple affair, attended by only the family and a few close friends. But the little man with the cane would remain in the hearts of moviegoers for many generations to come.

Charlie Chaplin's physical presence is gone, but his impact on movie history and the art of comedy is unforgettable. Perhaps Vatican Radio summarized it best when it reported, "Nobody as [Chaplin] did, knew how to enter the hidden recesses of the human heart with a simplicity and popularity which became legendary, succeeding in causing laughter by weeping, and weeping by laughter." Charlie Chaplin had built comedy into something warm and meaningful, infusing both characters and plots with tenderness. Characters such as the Tramp and the Kid touched the hearts of people of every age and background. As long as there are movie screens to show his films, Charlie Chaplin will continue to send his message to people all over the world.

Sources

27–28   John McCabe, *Charlie Chaplin* (Garden City, N.Y.: Doubleday & Co., 1978), 29.

28   Ibid., 32.

39   David Robinson, *Chaplin: His Life and Art* (New York: McGraw-Hill Book Company, 1985), 132.

52   Ibid., 252–253.

55   McCabe, *Charlie Chaplin,* 124.

61   Ibid., 156.

66   Jerry Epstein, *Remembering Charlie* (Garden City, N.Y.: Doubleday & Co., 1989), 25.

66–67   Ibid.

69   McCabe, *Charlie Chaplin,* 158.

72   Joyce Milton, *Tramp: The Life of Charlie Chaplin* (New York: HarperCollins, 1996), 349.

72   Kenneth S. Lynn, *Charlie Chaplin and His Times* (New York: Simon & Schuster, 1997), 369.

75   Ibid., 395.

77   Ibid., 406.

78   Robinson, *Chaplin,* 508.

78   McCabe, *Charlie Chaplin,* 196.

82   Ibid., 214.

82   Ibid.

86–87   Ibid., 223.

94   Ibid., 234.

94   Ibid., 235.

97   Lynn, *Charlie Chaplin and His Times,* 507.

101   McCabe, *Charlie Chaplin,* 243.

The Tramp throws himself into his work in Modern Times.

Bibliography

Asplund, Uno. *Chaplin's Films.* New York: A. S. Barnes and Company, 1976.

Chaplin, Charles. *My Autobiography.* New York: Simon & Schuster, 1964.

Cotes, Peter and Thelma Niklaus. *The Little Fellow.* Secaucus, N. J.: Citadel Press, 1965.

Epstein, Jerry. *Remembering Charlie.* Garden City, New York: Doubleday & Co., 1989.

Gerstein, David A. "The Chaplin Filmography." *Charlie Chaplin: A World Wide Web Celebration,* 1995. <http://wso.williams.edu/~ktaylor/ gerstein/chaplin/filmlist.html> (October 30, 1998).

Honri, Peter. *Working the Halls.* Hampshire, England: Saxon House, 1973.

Kerr, Walter. *The Silent Clowns.* New York: Alfred A. Knopf, 1975.

Lynn, Kenneth S. *Charlie Chaplin and His Times.* New York: Simon & Schuster, 1997.

McCabe, John. *Charlie Chaplin.* Garden City, New York: Doubleday & Co., 1978.

Milton, Joyce. *Tramp: The Life of Charlie Chaplin.* New York: HarperCollins, 1996.

Robinson, Davis. *Chaplin: His Life and Art.* New York: McGraw-Hill Book Company, 1985.

Schatz, Thomas. *The Genius of the System.* New York: Pantheon Books, 1988.

Taylor, Deems. *A Pictorial History of the Movies.* New York: Simon & Schuster, 1945.

Tyler, Parker. *Chaplin, Last of the Clowns.* New York: Horizon Press, 1972.

Filmography

All of Charlie Chaplin's eighty-one films are listed in chronological order under the name of the companies that released them. Chaplin made movies at five U.S. film companies before moving to Switzerland, where he produced his last two films independently.

Keystone Film Company

Making a Living

Kid Auto Races

Mabel's Strange Predicament

Between Showers

A Film Johnnie

Tango Tangles

His Favorite Pastime

Cruel, Cruel Love

The Star Boarder

Mabel at the Wheel

Twenty Minutes of Love

Caught in a Cabaret

Caught in the Rain

A Busy Day

The Fatal Mallet

Her Friend the Bandit

The Knockout

Mabel's Busy Day

Mabel's Married Life

Laughing Gas

The Property Man

The Face on the Barroom Floor

Recreation

The Masquerader

His New Profession

The Rounders

The New Janitor

Those Love Pangs

Dough and Dynamite

Gentlemen of Nerve

His Musical Career

His Trysting Place

Tillie's Punctured Romance

Getting Acquainted

His Prehistoric Past

Essanay Film Manufacturing Company

His New Job

A Night Out

The Champion

In the Park

A Jitney Elopement

The Tramp

By the Sea	*A Night in the Show*
Work	*Carmen*
A Woman	*Police!*
The Bank	*Triple Trouble*
Shanghaied	

Mutual Film Corporation

The Floorwalker	*Behind the Screen*
The Fireman	*The Rink*
The Vagabond	*Easy Street*
One A.M.	*The Cure*
The Count	*The Immigrant*
The Pawnshop	*The Adventurer*

First National Film Corporation

A Dog's Life	*The Kid*
Shoulder Arms	*The Idle Class*
The Bond	*Pay Day*
Sunnyside	*The Pilgrim*
A Day's Pleasure	

United Artists

A Woman of Paris	*Modern Times*
The Gold Rush	*The Great Dictator*
The Circus	*Monsier Verdoux*
City Lights	*Limelight*

Produced by Charlie Chaplin

The King in New York	*A Countess from Hong Kong*

Index

The Tramp tries to stay warm in The Gold Rush.

Charlie takes a look at a scene from the camera's point of view.

The Tramp pretends to be a priest in The Pilgrim.

Other Titles in the Lerner Biographies Series

Charlie and Paulette Goddard walk into the sunset in the final scene of Modern Times.

Photo Acknowledgments

The photographs and illustrations are reproduced with the permission of:
THE ILLUSTRATED LONDON NEWS PICTURE LIBRARY, 16, 24, 106;
AP/Wide World Photos, 2, 54, 60, 68, 80, 92, 98; Imapress/Archive Photos, 6,
32, 62, 111; The Art Institute of Chicago, 9; Corbis-Bettmann, 10, 12, 15, 30, 45,
67, 71, 72, 76 (left), 87; Popperfoto/Archive Photos, 20, 26, 109; UPI/Corbis-
Bettmann, 27, 48, 76 (right), 90; Corbis, 35; Photofest, 37, 40, 46, 82, 102, 107;
Brown Brothers, 43, 50, 51, 64, 95; Penguin/Corbis-Bettmann, 52; Archive
Photos, 56, 74, 79, 84, 96; John Springer/Corbis-Bettmann, 59; Horst
Tappe/Archive Photos, 89; Express Newspapers/Archive Photos, 99.

Cover, THE ILLUSTRATED LONDON NEWS PICTURE LIBRARY

About the Author

Ruth Turk—author, lecturer, columnist, and teacher—has been writing since the age of nine. Her first poem was published in the *New York Times* when she was ten. Since then, she has written books for both children and adults on a wide range of topics, including *The Play Is the Thing: A Story about William Shakespeare.* She has also worked as a teacher at the elementary, junior high, and high school levels. She lives with her husband in Florida.